Clean on the Inside

A Family Devotional for Holy Week

by

Erika Dawson

That a new generation will know ::
Our Redeemer LIVES!

Contents

Dear Friend,

I am so thankful for your desire to lead your family in reflecting on Jesus' death and resurrection this week.

I pray this devotional will not only help our families learn more about that final week of Jesus' life, but I pray it will elicit a response from us. May He speak to our hearts and move us to action that we might respond to Jesus, not just this week but for all of our lives.

How to Use this Book

This is a resource for you! Use it in the way that best fits your family. Depending on the age of your children, some modifications may need to be made.

I would recommend completing each day in the order it is listed, but depending on your schedule and the ages of your children, you might find it beneficial to pick and choose or to split the section up throughout the day.

To help younger children (or kids who are new to reading or listening to the Bible) understand the content, I would suggest reading the Bible passages from the New Living Translation, the International Children's Bible translation, or a children's Bible (see recommended resources for suggestions). Summarizing, rather than reading through the devotional portion, might also be helpful. Work within your child's attention span, but don't be afraid to stretch them a little!

Some days include multiple activities. Don't feel you need to complete them all and feel free to modify where necessary. These are simply suggested activities to help take the concept of the day one step further.

Do what works best for your family. This is not meant to be a strict format to follow but a tool to help you reflect and respond to Jesus this week.

May the power of Jesus' death and resurrection change each one of us!

Because of grace,

Erika Dawson

Erika Dawson
2012

As they approached Jerusalem and came to Bethphage on the Mount of Olives, Jesus sent two disciples, saying to them, "Go to the village ahead of you, and at once you will find a donkey tied there, with her colt by her. Untie them and bring them to me. If anyone says anything to you, say that the Lord needs them, and he will send them right away."

This took place to fulfill what was spoken through the prophet:

*"Say to Daughter Zion,
    'See, your king comes to you,
gentle and riding on a donkey,
    and on a colt, the foal of a donkey.'"*

The disciples went and did as Jesus had instructed them. They brought the donkey and the colt and placed their cloaks on them for Jesus to sit on. A very large crowd spread their cloaks on the road, while others cut branches from the trees and spread them on the road. The crowds that went ahead of him and those that followed shouted,

"Hosanna to the Son of David!"
"Blessed is he who comes in the name of the Lord!"
"Hosanna in the highest heaven!"

When Jesus entered Jerusalem, the whole city was stirred and asked, "Who is this?"

The crowds answered, "This is Jesus, the prophet from Nazareth in Galilee."

Matthew 21:1-11

Call on Jesus!

Palm Sunday: The Triumphal Entry

Bible Passage: Matthew 21:1-11

Additional Scripture: Zechariah 9:9

Have you ever needed help from someone? Maybe it was a problem you couldn't solve or a situation you couldn't fix on your own and you had to wait for someone to come and help you.

Let's imagine that you have a problem at school or in your playgroup. Maybe there are kids who aren't very nice to you. They might pick on you on the school bus or tease you on the playground. They take things from your desk or backpack when you're not looking, and they spread mean rumors about you to other kids.

Has that ever happened to you? Have you seen this happen to anyone else?

It would hurt, wouldn't it?

In a small way, that is what the Jewish people were facing. For thousands of years, the Israelites faced hardship. People were unkind to them, stealing their land and forcing them to be slaves. Others talked badly about the Jewish people and looked down on them.

The Roman government didn't give the Jews much freedom and life was really hard for them!

Even though they had walked a tough road, the Jewish people had hope! They had been promised a Messiah, someone who would come and save them!

It was kind of like being the kid who is picked on at the playground but knowing that one day a superhero would show up, and he'd be on *your* side.

The Israelites were waiting and watching and expecting a Savior! There were lots of stories and prophecies that told of this Savior's coming, and all of those stories were coming true in Jesus.

Though the Israelites were told that a king would come and save them, they were also informed that **he would be a king like no other. He would turn things upside down and inside out!** One of the signs of this special king was that he would come to his people riding on a donkey. Can you imagine that? A king, who should have been carried on a brightly decorated chariot, entered Jerusalem riding on a lowly beast of burden. By now, you've probably guessed that this king was none other than Jesus.

The people were so excited as He entered the Holy City. They were shouting "Hosanna," which means "Save us!" and they waved palm branches (something the people would do to welcome a new political leader). The Jews welcomed Jesus as their king and expected that the Kingdom of God was going to appear immediately! They were looking to Jesus, calling on Him to save them from the Roman government — to save them *right now*!

But Jesus wasn't coming to save them just from the Roman government. **He had a *much bigger* plan and a much harder mission.** One that only He could complete.

Some of the people didn't recognize the signs, and many didn't understand until later, but the out-of-this-world news was that **Jesus was sent as their Messiah to deliver them, not from the harsh treatment of the Romans, but from a much worse enemy... sin.**

Jesus came to save us, too! Will we respond to His invitation?

Talk about it:

For the Kids:

- Start your conversation with a simple "I wonder" statement, like, "I wonder: What would I have shouted at Jesus as He rode by" or "I wonder: Why does Jesus want to be my king?" Give time for the kids to share their own "I wonder" statements or ask any questions they might have.

- Ask a few questions to continue the conversation ::

  o Why do we need a Savior? (to save us from our sins)

  o Have you ever sinned? (Yes, the Bible tells us that all have sinned.)

  o What are some things you have done that are sin? (disobeying, hitting my brother, not telling the truth)

  o When you do some of those things, how do you feel? (bad, angry, trapped, out-of-control, etc. Talk about how that "bad" feeling is because of sin in our lives. Discuss how we all sin and that sin separates us from God. We need a Savior who can save us from our sins and restore a right relationship with God. Jesus is our Savior, and we can call on Him!)

- End with a prayer, thanking Jesus for being our Savior.

For Us:

Do we recognize our need for a Savior? Are we putting all of our hope and trust in Jesus to save us, or are we trying to do it on our own? Are we expecting Jesus to save us just from our circumstances, or do we understand that He might have a greater purpose in allowing us to experience those circumstances?

Activities:

Put it into Action:

- Re-enact Jesus' triumphal entry! Designate someone to be the donkey, someone to be Jesus, and the rest of the family to cheer, shouting "Hosanna!" and laying coats down to pave the way.

- During the triumphal entry, Luke records Jesus as saying that if the people were silent and didn't praise Him, the very rocks would cry out with praise! Gather some rocks or boulders and paint them with words of praise. You might use words from today's Scripture reading —"Hosanna!" "Blessed is He!" — or choose other words you would use to praise Jesus.

Remember It:

Memorize John 3:16-17.

> *For God so loved the world that he gave his one and only Son, that whoever believes in him shall not perish but have eternal life. For God did not send his Son into the world to condemn the world, but to save the world through him.*
> John 3:16-17

F   G   s   l   t   w   t   h   g   h   o   a   o   S,   t   w

b   i   h   s   n   p   b   h   e   l.   F   G   d   n   s   h

S   i   t   w   t   c   t   w,   b   t   s   t   w   t   h.

_____ _____ : _____ – _____

Jesus entered the temple courts and drove out all who were buying and selling there. He overturned the tables of the money changers and the benches of those selling doves. "It is written," he said to them, "'My house will be called a house of prayer,'but you are making it 'a den of robbers.'"

The blind and the lame came to him at the temple, and he healed them. But when the chief priests and the teachers of the law saw the wonderful things he did and the children shouting in the temple courts, "Hosanna to the Son of David," they were indignant.

"Do you hear what these children are saying?" they asked him.

"Yes," replied Jesus, "have you never read,

"'From the lips of children and infants
*   you, Lord, have called forth your praise'?"*
And he left them and went out of the city to Bethany, where he spent the night.

Matthew 21:12-17

Honor Jesus!

Monday – The Cleansing of the Temple

Bible Passage: Matthew 21:12-17

Additional Scripture: 1 Corinthians 6:19-20

The day after Jesus entered Jerusalem riding on a donkey, he visited the Temple. If you don't know much about the Temple, let me tell you, it was a very important place. If people wanted to worship God, they couldn't just talk to God like we do, they had to go to the temple where a priest would talk to God for them.

They couldn't simply ask God to forgive them if they did something wrong, they had to go to the Temple and offer sacrifices. The rules were very strict and the laws were not to be broken, even by the priests. That was because, **until Jesus died, the temple contained the very presence of God, who is holy and perfect.**

The temple was so important that God gave very detailed instructions to the Jewish people about everything that was to take place there. Sadly, **in those days, however, it looked more like a three-ring circus than a special place to worship the Lord!** There were people there who were taking advantage of those who came to offer their sacrifices.

Instead of carrying out God's orders, they set up booths inside the temple to earn a high profit by selling special "temple animals" and "temple money" that were to be given to God. These sellers weren't trying to help the people, they were trying to make a lot of money! In doing this they were cheating the people and robbing God, but even worse, they were defiling God's holy temple! **They were not honoring Him!**

When Jesus showed up on that first Palm Sunday and saw all of this, He would not stand for it! To make matters worse, He had already told them once before that what they were doing was wrong (John 2:12-125). He came in to the temple and turned the tables upside down and chased the cheaters and robbers out!

God's temple was to be holy and pure because before Jesus died, it was God's dwelling place. Back then, the people worshiped God in a temple, sort of like how we worship God in a church building today. But the great news is that because Jesus died and rose again, we can worship God anywhere!

Jesus came and cleansed the temple, but more importantly, **He came to cleanse us from the inside out so that we could become His temple, the place where God lives!**

Jesus came to save us from our sins so that not only could we be friends with God, but so that God could live inside of us! We are now the temple of God!

Talk about it:

For the Kids:

- How do you know if God's Spirit lives inside of you? (This is a great opportunity to share the Gospel with the kids! Everyone who believes in Jesus for salvation receives the promised Holy Spirit!) Do you have God's Spirit living inside of you?

- How do we listen more to God's Spirit who lives in us? (Reading the Bible, praying, obeying God's Word, etc.)

- If Jesus lives in us, we should take care of our physical bodies, but we should also take care of our spiritual bodies. What are ways we take care of our physical bodies? What about our spiritual bodies? What changes do we need to make to show honor to Jesus through our bodies?

- How can we honor God when we go to church? What are some things we can do to show God respect?

For us:

- What are the attitudes of our hearts as we come to church on Sunday morning? Have we prepared our hearts? Are we looking only for what we can "get" out of church? Are there any attitudes or hardened hearts that we need to confess and surrender to Jesus?

- Of course we should take care of our physical bodies by eating nourishing food, getting proper amounts of exercise, and practicing good hygiene, but if Jesus lives in us, we have to take care of our spiritual bodies too. Think about how you care for your spiritual body. What are you watching, listening to, participating in, saying, and thinking about? Are we honoring God in how we care for our spiritual bodies? Are we taking care of these "temples"? Take time to confess any wrong attitudes, activities, or mindsets you've been stuck in.

- Are we cheating God by living for ourselves, or are we living for Him?

Activities:

Put it into Action:

- As a family, decorate a place in your home to worship during Holy Week. Include a Bible, this devotional, some quiet music, and some candles or a soft lamp. Take time throughout the week to reflect on what role we play in the church. Are we honoring God with our attitudes and behaviors at church? Think also about how we are using our bodies. We, who are believers, are the temple of the holy God! Are we honoring God with our bodies?

Remember It:

Memorize Galatians 5:16, 22-23.

> *But I say, walk by the Spirit, and you will not gratify the desires of the flesh.*
>
> *...*
>
> *But the fruit of the Spirit is love, joy, peace, patience, kindness, goodness, faithfulness, gentleness, self-control; against such things there is no law.*
> Galatians 5:16, 22-23 ESV

B   I   s,   w   b   t   S,   a   y   w   n   g   t   d   o

t   f .

B   t   f   o   t   S   i   l,   j,   p,   p,   k,   g,   f,

g   a   s - c;   a   s   t   t   i   n   l .

_____ _____ : _____ , _____ - _____

"Woe to you, teachers of the law and Pharisees, you hypocrites! You clean the outside of the cup and dish, but inside they are full of greed and self-indulgence. Blind Pharisee! First clean the inside of the cup and dish, and then the outside also will be clean.

"Woe to you, teachers of the law and Pharisees, you hypocrites! You are like whitewashed tombs, which look beautiful on the outside but on the inside are full of the bones of the dead and everything unclean. In the same way, on the outside you appear to people as righteous but on the inside you are full of hypocrisy and wickedness.

Matthew 23:25-28

Abide in Jesus!

Tuesday – Whitewashed Tombs

Bible Passage: Matthew 23:25-28

Additional Scripture: Isaiah 29:13, John 15:4-5, Galatians 3:2-4

The week that Jesus was in Jerusalem, he spent a lot of time telling stories and teaching people about God. The Jewish people, especially the religious leaders believed that if they acted good enough and kept God's law, they would be loved by God. Jesus taught differently, though. He told the people that while **what is on the outside is important, so is what is on the inside, in our hearts and minds.** We can do right things, but if the attitude in our hearts is ugly, we may well be sinning.

That is why Jesus scolded the religious leaders. He told them that **even though on the outside they *looked* righteous and appeared to be keeping the law, inside, their hearts were dirty and full of ugliness.** While their actions might have been okay, their attitudes were all wrong.

It's kind of like when you ooh and awe over a beautiful cake that has been left out on the counter for many days. The frosting looks sweet and the decorations look pretty, but when you cut into it, you find that it's dry and crusty and growing mold. You can only hide behind a beautiful exterior for so long. **The inside always comes out.**

Jesus used even stronger words to teach the same lesson. He said that these religious leaders were like tombs where dead people are buried! The outsides of the tombs are cleaned and decorated to look attractive, but inside is death and decay!

It is a lot easier to appear holy than it is to actually *be* holy. **We might be able to fool people, but we can't hide anything from God.** He knows us better than we know ourselves!. He even knows our thoughts before we think them! God is not interested in our behaviors alone, He's interested in our motives. God looks on the inside. He looks at our hearts.

Even if we try our hardest, we can never be perfect on our own. We can never meet God's standard of holiness. We need a Savior to cleanse us from the inside out by forgiving our sins. That is what Jesus came to do. He came to clean our hearts!

Once we allow Jesus to clean the inside, we must *abide in Him* so that the outside will start to become beautiful, too.

Talk about it:

For the Kids:

- What are some things God tells us we are to do? (obey our parents, be kind to others, do everything without complaining or arguing, etc.)

- How does He want us to do these things? (with a good attitude, cheerfully)

- Discuss how difficult this is sometimes. It's hard to always obey joyfully, but when Jesus cleans our heart from sin, He moves in! He can help us do these things with a good attitude, but we have to ask Him to help.

- What are some things we can do when we are struggling to obey or have a good attitude? (pray, remember a verse, sing a song)

- Discuss what it means to "spend time with Jesus" and how spending time with Jesus helps prepare us for those hard times.

- What are some things you can do to spend time with Jesus? (read the Bible, pray, memorize verses, etc.)

For us:

- Even if our actions are right, if the motives of our heart are wrong, those ugly motives can harden our hearts and weigh us down. What are some examples of having right actions but wrong motives?

- In order to have sweet fruit in our lives, we need to abide in Christ! Do I spend time with Jesus so that He can refine me and grow the fruit of the Spirit in my life or am I striving to live a certain way just because that is how a Christian is supposed to live?

- What do I need to surrender or change to allow Jesus to cleanse me from the inside out?

Activities:

- Fill a clear drinking glass or jar with water and add a few drops of food coloring to make the water appear dark.

- Give your child(ren) a small cup of clear water. Standing over a large bowl or sink, have the kids take turns pouring cupfuls of clear water into the drinking glass filled with dark water so that the clear water begins to dilute and overflow the dark water out of the glass. Continue to pour more clear water into the darkened glass until that water is also completely clear.

- Explain that when we turn to Jesus and confess our sins, He is faithful to forgive us and cleanse us from all unrighteousness (1 John 1:9). When God fills us with His Spirit, He cleanses the sinful, dark areas of our lives and places within us His light and righteousness. As we abide in the Spirit, His fruit grows in our lives!

Remember It:

Memorize John 15:5.

I am the vine; you are the branches. Whoever abides in me and I in him, he it is that bears much fruit, for apart from me you can do nothing.

John 15:5 ESV

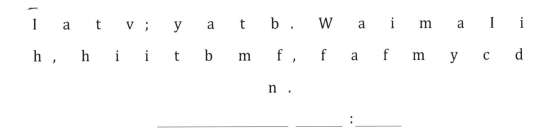

While Jesus was in Bethany in the home of Simon the Leper, a woman came to him with an alabaster jar of very expensive perfume, which she poured on his head as he was reclining at the table.

When the disciples saw this, they were indignant. "Why this waste?" they asked. "This perfume could have been sold at a high price and the money given to the poor."

Aware of this, Jesus said to them, "Why are you bothering this woman? She has done a beautiful thing to me. The poor you will always have with you, but you will not always have me. When she poured this perfume on my body, she did it to prepare me for burial. Truly I tell you, wherever this gospel is preached throughout the world, what she has done will also be told, in memory of her."

Then one of the Twelve—the one called Judas Iscariot—went to the chief priests and asked, "What are you willing to give me if I deliver him over to you?" So they counted out for him thirty pieces of silver. From then on Judas watched for an opportunity to hand him over.

Matthew 26:6-16

Give to Jesus!

Wednesday — Jesus anointed by Mary

Bible Passage: Matthew 26:6-16

Additional Scripture: Zechariah 11:13, Mark 14:3-11, John 12:1-8

If you were to stand in the middle of a room holding a full glass of water, and I knocked your arm, what would happen? The water would slosh out over the top of the glass and spill on the floor, right? You might get mad and say that the mess was my fault because I bumped into you. Or you might get mad, complaining that the water spilled because there was no lid on the glass, but either way, the one thing we know for sure is that what was inside the glass is now outside the glass. The *cause* of the spill didn't change what spilled out. **What is on the inside always comes out, one way or another.**

Today we are going to look at two people whose lives were shaken by Jesus. What spills out of their hearts and onto others is very different for each.

During Jesus' last days, the religious and political rulers of the Jews were making plans to arrest Him. **They worried that they might lose their power and positions if the people recognized Jesus as their Messiah.** Meanwhile Jesus continued to spend time with his friends.

While eating dinner with the disciples at a man named Simon's home, a woman named Mary came to visit. Mary was a woman who *loved* Jesus. **He had changed her life, and her heart was devoted to him. This showed in her actions.**

When Mary arrived, she went to Jesus and poured a very expensive oil over his head and feet and even cleaned Jesus' feet with her hair. The oil was very expensive and cost as much as the average person earned working for an entire year! Mary sacrificed financially, giving the best of what she had, to show her love and devotion to Jesus. **It didn't matter what it cost her!**

Another person who was there that same night, however, didn't have the same attitude.

Judas, one of Jesus' disciples, had the job of taking care of the money for his friends. He had a problem with greed, though, and often stole money from the moneybag. **He was blinded by his own sin and was disgusted by Mary's gift to Jesus.** He said that it was a waste and the oil should have been sold and given to the poor.

Even though that *sounded* like the right thing to do, Judas didn't really care about the poor. He was only focused on his own selfish gain and didn't see the greater purpose in Mary's gift – one that she wasn't even aware of at that time. Anointing Jesus with oil was a way of preparing His body for burial that would come in just a few short days after he had died.

Mary was obeying what God put in her heart, even though she didn't fully understand and even though it looked foolish to others. Her love for Jesus compelled her to give to Him. By doing so, Mary fulfilled a prophecy and demonstrated that she had been cleaned from the inside out.

Judas tried to be clean on the outside without a thought to what was inside. Sin kept him blind to the truth so that he ended up betraying Jesus for just thirty pieces of silver.

Mary gave all she had to show her devotion to Jesus, but Judas took what he could to betray Him.

Talk about it:

For the Kids:

- Explain that when we love someone, we often show our love by *doing* things for them and *giving* them things. Love is an action, and it is the same way with Jesus! He loved us so much that He died on the cross to save us from the eternal death we would face because of our sin. Every day, God gives us *so many* good gifts. What are some of the gifts God has given *us*?

- How do you feel about what God did for you through Jesus? In what ways do you want to say thank you and show Him that you love Him?

- Talk about how when we give to others because we love God, that is a way to give back to Him. How can we show love to God by loving others?

For Us:

- Does our love for Jesus compel *us* to give?

- Are we willing to give *the best* of what we have?

- What are we clinging to that Jesus might be asking us to give away (time, possessions, relationship, etc.)?

Activities:

Put it into Action:

- Discuss something that you can give up and give away individually or as a family. Don't just give the old, worn-out and used stuff, give sacrificially. Now go out and do it!

Remember It:

Memorize 2 Corinthians 5:14-15.

For the love of Christ controls us, because we have concluded this: that one has died for all, therefore all have died; and he died for all, that those who live might no longer live for themselves but for him who for their sake died and was raised.

2 Corinthians 5:14-15 ESV

F t l o C c u , b w h c t : t o h

d f a , t a h d ; a h d f a , t t w

l m n l l f t b f h w f t s d a

w r .

_ _____ _____ :_____ - _____

On the first day of the Festival of Unleavened Bread, the disciples came to Jesus and asked, "Where do you want us to make preparations for you to eat the Passover?"

He replied, "Go into the city to a certain man and tell him, 'The Teacher says: My appointed time is near. I am going to celebrate the Passover with my disciples at your house.'" So the disciples did as Jesus had directed them and prepared the Passover.

When evening came, Jesus was reclining at the table with the Twelve. And while they were eating, he said, "Truly I tell you, one of you will betray me."

They were very sad and began to say to him one after the other, "Surely you don't mean me, Lord?"

Jesus replied, "The one who has dipped his hand into the bowl with me will betray me. The Son of Man will go just as it is written about him. But woe to that man who betrays the Son of Man! It would be better for him if he had not been born."

Then Judas, the one who would betray him, said, "Surely you don't mean me, Rabbi?"

Jesus answered, "You have said so."

While they were eating, Jesus took bread, and when he had given thanks, he broke it and gave it to his disciples, saying, "Take and eat; this is my body."

Then he took a cup, and when he had given thanks, he gave it to them, saying, "Drink from it, all of you. This is my blood of the covenant, which is poured out for many for the forgiveness of sins. I tell you, I will not drink from this fruit of the vine from now on until that day when I drink it new with you in my Father's kingdom."

When they had sung a hymn, they went out to the Mount of Olives.

Matthew 26:17-30

Serve Jesus!

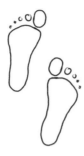

Thursday – Passover

Bible Passage: Matthew 26:17-30

Additional Scripture: John 13:1-20, Hebrews 10:19-22

Does your family have any special traditions that help you remember certain events? Maybe every year on your birthday your family wakes you up by singing "Happy Birthday." Or maybe you have a tradition of eating cinnamon rolls for breakfast every New Year's Day.

The Feast of Passover was an important tradition for the Jewish people to keep, but in reality, **it was much more than just a tradition**.

Celebrating the Passover was something God commanded the people to do. It was to be a reminder to the Jewish people every year, for generations and generations, that God saved them when they were slaves in Egypt. God delivered His people from the hands of the Egyptians, but He also delivered them from one of the worst plagues that God sent on Egypt.

That last plague was a very serious one. To be protected from it, God told the Israelites to sacrifice a lamb and cover the doorposts of their homes with the lamb's blood. If they obeyed and did what God said, the plague would actually pass over them, and they wouldn't be affected by it. **The Passover meal is celebrated every single year to remind the Jewish people that God saved His people!**

Jesus ate the Passover meal with his disciples because it was a very important custom of his people, but there was also an even bigger meaning behind it. *Jesus* **was about to become the Passover lamb!** By dying on the cross, perfect, innocent Jesus was about to become our sacrifice, taking our sins upon himself that we might be set free from sin and even death. **Through Jesus, God was about to provide salvation for the whole world!**

As they were eating the Passover meal, Jesus did something radical. He did what only a servant would normally do.

He knelt before the disciples, grasped their dirty and stinky feet in His hands and washed them. Jesus showed them that *He is the only way to be clean*! **The only way to have a**

friendship with God is to be washed by Jesus.

The Bible reminds us that all have sinned and fall short of God's standards, and the *only* way for us to know God and spend eternity with Him is through Jesus making us clean by forgiving us from our sins. He is the only One who can make a person clean on the inside.

Through washing His disciples' feet, however, **Jesus was setting an example for us to follow,** even today. Just as King Jesus, who deserves all honor and glory, got down on His knees and served the disciples by washing their feet, so we are to serve one another. Jesus set an example for us. **We are to serve Jesus by serving one another.**

Talk about it:

For the Kids:

- Jesus tells us that one of the ways we serve Him is by serving others (Matthew 25:31-46). What are some ways we can serve others and show God that we love Him?

- Serving others doesn't come naturally to most of us. What areas are the hardest for you to think of others before thinking of yourself? How can you grow in that area this month?

- 1 Corinthians 10:31 tells us, "So whether you eat or drink or whatever you do, do it all for the glory of God." How can this verse help us in how, when, and why we serve others?

For us:

- Are we willing to die to ourselves that we might serve the Lord?

- Are we willing to serve Jesus by serving others?

- Reflect on Philippians 2:1-11. In what area do you struggle most with "selfish ambition," and have a hard time putting other people's needs ahead of your own? Confess this to the Lord. Begin memorizing verses three and four and ask God to help you apply these verse in your own life.

Activities:

Put it into Action:

- As a family, wash one another's feet. Set out basins of warm, soapy water. Have a quiet time of reflection as you wash each other's feet. Give each person an opportunity to serve someone in the family by washing their feet. Discuss how it felt to serve and how it felt to be served.

Remember It:

Memorize Matthew 20:26b-28.

... whoever would be great among you must be your servant, and whoever would be first among you must be your slave, even as the Son of Man came not to be served but to serve, and to give his life as a ransom for many.

Matthew 20:26b - 28 ESV

. . .   w   w   b   g   a   y   m   b   y   s ,   a   w   w

b   f   a   y   m   b   y   s ,   e   a   t   S   o   M   c   n

t   b   s   b   t   s ,   a   t   g   h   l   a   a   r   f   m .

_____ _____ : _____ - _____

While they were eating, Jesus took bread, and when he had given thanks, he broke it and gave it to his disciples, saying, "Take and eat; this is my body."

Then he took a cup, and when he had given thanks, he gave it to them, saying, "Drink from it, all of you. This is my blood of the[a] covenant, which is poured out for many for the forgiveness of sins. I tell you, I will not drink from this fruit of the vine from now on until that day when I drink it new with you in my Father's kingdom."

When they had sung a hymn, they went out to the Mount of Olives.

—

Then the governor's soldiers took Jesus into the Praetorium and gathered the whole company of soldiers around him. They stripped him and put a scarlet robe on him, and then twisted together a crown of thorns and set it on his head. They put a staff in his right hand. Then they knelt in front of him and mocked him. "Hail, king of the Jews!" they said. They spit on him, and took the staff and struck him on the head again and again. After they had mocked him, they took off the robe and put his own clothes on him. Then they led him away to crucify him.

—

From noon until three in the afternoon darkness came over all the land. About three in the afternoon Jesus cried out in a loud voice, "Eli, Eli, lema sabachthani?" (which means "My God, my God, why have you forsaken me?").

When some of those standing there heard this, they said, "He's calling Elijah."

Immediately one of them ran and got a sponge. He filled it with wine vinegar, put it on a staff, and offered it to Jesus to drink. The rest said, "Now leave him alone. Let's see if Elijah comes to save him."

And when Jesus had cried out again in a loud voice, he gave up his spirit.

At that moment the curtain of the temple was torn in two from top to bottom. The earth shook, the rocks split and the tombs broke open. The bodies of many holy people who had died were raised to life. They came out of the tombs after Jesus' resurrection and[c] went into the holy city and appeared to many people.

When the centurion and those with him who were guarding Jesus saw the earthquake and all that had happened, they were terrified, and exclaimed, "Surely he was the Son of God!"

Matthew 26:26-30 & Matthew 27:27-31, 45-54

Remember Jesus!

Friday – Good Friday

Bible Passage: Matthew 26:26-30, 27:27-31, 27:45-54

Additional Scripture: Isaiah 53:5-6, Romans 5:8

We have talked all week about how Jesus is the only way to have a relationship with God. **He is the only One who can clean out the sin in our hearts and lives, but sometimes we forget that.** We try really hard to make ourselves look good to others and earn the approval of God and our friends.

Jesus knew we would have a hard time remembering. That's why during the Passover meal, **Jesus gave the disciples something to *do* to always remember Jesus.** It is something we call Communion. It is a reminder that *Jesus* is the one who saves us. Out of His great love for us, He came as a king like none other, humbled Himself, and died for our sins. That is what today is all about.

After Jesus and the disciples finished eating the Passover meal, they went to a place called Gethsemane, a large garden with lots of olive trees. While there, **Jesus spent a long time in prayer.** His heart was heavy with concern — for what was about to happen and for these disciples that he loved.

Even though Jesus was the Son of God, spending time in prayer with His Heavenly Father was very important to Him. **Jesus knew that what he was about to face on the cross would be the most physically, emotionally, and spiritually painful thing any one could and would ever face.** He poured out his heart to his Father asking if there was another way to accomplish this mission, to save the world.

After much prayer, Jesus knew that the only way to save His followers was to offer Himself as the sacrifice for their sins, so He accepted that this was His Father's will and prepared Himself for what was to come.

After Jesus had finished praying, Judas, one of the twelve disciples, the one who betrayed Jesus, led a great crowd to come and capture Jesus.

You might be wondering why Jesus was arrested when he had never done anything wrong.

It was the religious leaders of the Jewish people who were out to get Jesus. They accused Jesus of *blasphemy*, saying that he was stealing glory from God by claiming to actually *be* God. Whoever committed blasphemy was guilty of breaking the first commandment, and according to the Law of Moses, was to be punished by death. These were really serious accusations to be spoken against any person, but not at Jesus because He really was the Son of God! In admitting this, He did nothing wrong.

The Jewish religious leaders and their politicians put Jesus on trial that day. They found Him guilty of claiming to be God and then turned Him over to the Roman governor so that He might be sentenced to death.

When Pontius Pilate, the Roman governor questioned Jesus, however, he couldn't find any reason to punish Him. Though he believed that Jesus was innocent, Pilate asked the large crowd of people that had gathered to watch what they thought he should do.

The crowd was shouting to crucify Jesus, to kill him, so Pilate gave in and sentenced Jesus to death.

Can you imagine being punished for something you didn't even do? Jesus knew he was innocent but he didn't even defend himself! He knew that all of these things had to happen so that he could save us from our sin. **Jesus came to make us clean from the inside out and was willing to do whatever was necessary to make it happen.**

A short time later, Jesus was beaten and made fun of; he was tortured and spit on. People yelled and screamed at him.

Even though the Roman soldiers nailed Him to the cross, it wasn't the torture that killed him. The Bible tells us that **Jesus willingly "gave up His spirit." He allowed himself to die.** God who is our righteous judge, put the sin of the world on Jesus because he was a perfect sacrifice. He alone could pay the penalty for our sins.

Jesus became the lamb that was sacrificed for *our* sins. He took *our* punishment and died in *our* place!

As a church, we celebrate communion as a reminder of what Jesus did for us. May we never forget the Lamb of God who sacrificed Himself to save us!

Talk about it:

For the Kids:

- Discuss together Jesus' death. How does it make you feel? Why was it so important? How does it change us?

- Help your child to think about how Jesus' death changes their future!

- Take time to reflect on the sacrifice Jesus made. What did He save you from? What would your life be like apart from Christ?

Activities:

Put it into Action:

- **Nail it to the cross:** Make a cross out of wood scraps. Ask each family member to think of an attitude or action from the past week that they knew didn't make God happy. Have family members write their thoughts on a piece of paper, fold it and pin it to the cross. Talk about how Jesus suffered the punishment for all of our sins so that we would not have to.

- **Easter Basket with Rocks activity:**

  1. Gather a bunch of rocks from outside and discuss how rocks are like sin, weighing us down. The more we sin, the harder our hearts become, eventually leading to a heart of stone.

  2. Talk about the various sins we each struggle with personally and write them on the rocks and put them in the basket.

  3. Cover the basket with a red piece of cloth to represent Jesus' death. He shed His blood to cover all of our sins, to change our hearts of stone to hearts of flesh (Ezekiel 36:26), and to clean us on the inside. Leave the basket covered until the following morning (or until Resurrection Day).

  4. Without the children, remove the rocks and place in a new rock, one with Jesus' name on it. When they return to their baskets and remove the red cloth, they will find that their basket of sins is no longer there! Jesus has taken their sins away! Take time to pray and celebrate this marvelous gift together.

Remember It:

Memorize Romans 5:8.

but God shows his love for us in that while we were still sinners, Christ died for us.

Romans 5:8 ESV

b   G   s   h   l   f   u   i   t   w   w   w   s   s ,   C   d   f   u .

_____   _____ : _____

As evening approached, there came a rich man from Arimathea, named Joseph, who had himself become a disciple of Jesus. Going to Pilate, he asked for Jesus' body, and Pilate ordered that it be given to him. Joseph took the body, wrapped it in a clean linen cloth, and placed it in his own new tomb that he had cut out of the rock. He rolled a big stone in front of the entrance to the tomb and went away. Mary Magdalene and the other Mary were sitting there opposite the tomb.

The next day, the one after Preparation Day, the chief priests and the Pharisees went to Pilate. "Sir," they said, "we remember that while he was still alive that deceiver said, 'After three days I will rise again.' So give the order for the tomb to be made secure until the third day. Otherwise, his disciples may come and steal the body and tell the people that he has been raised from the dead. This last deception will be worse than the first."

"Take a guard," Pilate answered. "Go, make the tomb as secure as you know how." So they went and made the tomb secure by putting a seal on the stone and posting the guard.

Matthew 27:57-66

Trust Jesus!

Saturday – Buried

Bible Passage: Matthew 27:57-66

Additional Scripture: Isaiah 53:12

The same evening Jesus died, a man named Joseph from the town of Arimathea, asked Pilate for permission to bury Jesus' body. His body was tightly wrapped in a linen covering and was laid in a brand new tomb, one that had been cut into a rock. A great stone was placed in front of the entrance, and Roman soldiers stood guard in front of the stone.

Have you ever had to face the death of someone you loved? If so, you know how it felt for the disciples. Jesus was their best friend, their teacher and role model, but he was also their Savior. **All of their hopes were resting on him, and when he was crucified, they didn't understand why!** They were so disappointed and heartbroken because they didn't understand Jesus' great mission.

The Bible teaches that the wages of sin is death. By going to the cross, Jesus died to pay the penalty for our sins. This had been His mission all along. That's why Jesus' very last words were: "It is finished," but to the disciples, it looked like the great plan was sabotaged.

It looked like the end.

Isn't that usually what death is: the end? But the disciples had a choice, they could trust all of the words and teachings and promises of Jesus or they could give up in despair.

The disciples had to trust Jesus even when they didn't understand what He was allowing to happen.

Talk about it

For the Kids:

- How would you have felt if you had been there when Jesus died?

- What would you have done?

- When we don't understand what Jesus is doing in our lives, why should we trust Him?

- What are some things we can do to help us trust Him?

- Are you walking through any trials, struggling to understand what God is doing and why He is allowing certain things to happen? Take time to reflect on the character of God and admit your dependence on Him. Use Psalm 43:5 to begin a time of prayer and sharing your heart with God.

Activities:

Put it into Action:

- Take turns wrapping each other in toilet paper to look like Jesus might have when He was prepared to be buried. Use the discussion questions above to talk about how the disciples might have felt when all their hopes seemed destroyed when Jesus died.

- Try to look through a dirty window or see an image in a dusty mirror. Discuss how difficult it is to see clearly. Now work with your kids to clean the surface. Discuss how much better they can see afterward and how much clearer the view is. Read Luke 18:31-34. Explain that the disciples did not see clearly at first. They did not understand that Jesus had to die and rise from the dead — until He did!

Remember It:

Memorize Proverbs 3:5-6.

Trust in the Lord with all your heart, and do not lean on your own understanding. In all your ways acknowledge him, and he will make straight your paths.

Proverbs 3:5-6 ESV

T   i   t   L   w   a   y   h   ,   a   d   n   l   o   y   o

u   .   I   a   y   w   a   h   ,   a   h   w   m   s   y   p   .

_____ _____ : _____ - _____

For God so loved the world that he gave his one and only Son, that whoever believes in him shall not perish but have eternal life.

John 3:16

After the Sabbath, at dawn on the first day of the week, Mary Magdalene and the other Mary went to look at the tomb.

There was a violent earthquake, for an angel of the Lord came down from heaven and, going to the tomb, rolled back the stone and sat on it. His appearance was like lightning, and his clothes were white as snow. 4 The guards were so afraid of him that they shook and became like dead men.

The angel said to the women, "Do not be afraid, for I know that you are looking for Jesus, who was crucified. He is not here; he has risen, just as he said. Come and see the place where he lay. Then go quickly and tell his disciples: 'He has risen from the dead and is going ahead of you into Galilee. There you will see him.' Now I have told you."

So the women hurried away from the tomb, afraid yet filled with joy, and ran to tell his disciples. Suddenly Jesus met them. "Greetings," he said. They came to him, clasped his feet and worshiped him. Then Jesus said to them, "Do not be afraid. Go and tell my brothers to go to Galilee; there they will see me."

Matthew 28:1-10

Live for Jesus!

Resurrection Sunday – He's ALIVE!

Bible Passage: Matthew 28:1-10, John 3:16

Additional Scripture: Mark 16:1-8, Luke 24:1-12, John 20:1-18

Can you imagine losing someone you love? How would you feel? What would you do? If you were walking to the gravesite, you would probably walk slowly with your head down and your eyes filled with tears. You probably wouldn't talk much and smiling would be far from your mind.

That is how the women felt as they went to visit Jesus' tomb. They went early in the morning before anyone else. When they arrived at the tomb, however, they had the shock of their lives!

There was a great earthquake and an angel appeared from heaven and rolled back the huge stone in front of the tomb. Then he proclaimed the good news: the angel told the women that Jesus wasn't there – he was alive! He had risen, just like he said he would!

Jesus was alive!

This meant that **everything He said to His disciples was true**! Jesus had taken all of our ugliness and sin on Himself when He died on the cross, and then **He conquered death itself by rising from the grave.** He died but became alive again showing that **he is God and he has power even over death!**

Because of *His* resurrection, death is not the end. *We* can have hope for new life and live with Jesus forever! We don't have to be slaves to sin. Because of His resurrection, everyone who puts their trust in Jesus has life, abundant and eternal. We are no longer condemned to be slaves of sin. We don't have to try to make ourselves acceptable to God. Jesus did it all when He died and rose from the grave.

God so loved the world that He gave his one and only Son that whoever believes in Him will not die but will live with Him forever. Jesus is our Hosanna! Amen!

Talk about it:

For the Kids:

- Take time to celebrate the good news of Jesus' death and resurrection. Make it a party and discuss why we can rejoice!

- Read and discuss John 11:25-26 together and reflect on the question Jesus asks :: "Jesus said to her, 'I am the resurrection and the life. Whoever believes in me, though he die, yet shall he live, and everyone who lives and believes in me shall never die. Do you believe this?'"

- Explain that when Jesus ascended into Heaven, He sent the Holy Spirit as our helper.

  - Does every person have the Holy Spirit? (No, only those who trust Jesus for salvation)

  - When do we need the help of the Holy Spirit? (Discuss how our lives can be different because of Jesus' death and resurrection and the Holy Spirit living inside of us.)

For Us:

- Colossians 3:1 tells us that we were raised with Christ! What do you think these words mean?

- What about Colossians 3:3-4: "For you died, and your life is now hidden with Christ in God. When Christ, who is your life, appears, then you also will appear with Him in glory." What does it mean for Christ to be our life? How can this impact our day-to-day lives, especially when faced with trials and temptations? Take time to reflect on and pray for a deeper understanding of what it means to be "raised with Christ" and live a life "hidden with Christ in God."

- If we have accepted Jesus as our Savior, we have the Holy Spirit living within us. The same power that raised Christ from the dead is living in us! In what ways have we experienced the new life that Jesus came to give us through His death and resurrection? Are there any areas of bondage that we have yet to "crucify with Christ"? Take time to confess any areas of sin or self-dependence and ask the Holy Spirit to work through you that you might live in victory over these sins and habits.

- Reflect on the hope we have in Christ, that though our earthly bodies will die, we will live forever with Jesus!

Activities:

Put it into Action:

- Hide candy-filled eggs for a fun-filled egg hunt. Make sure to hide one egg that is empty. Whoever finds the empty egg should call out, "He's not here! He has risen, just as he said!" Whoever finds the empty egg wins a prize! (idea from Thriving Family magazine March/April 2011)

- Open Easter story cookies (from optional activities). They are hollow! On the first Easter, Jesus' followers were amazed to find the tomb open and empty. Read Matthew 28:1-9. **HE HAS RISEN!**

- As you celebrate Resurrection Sunday today, share together what you have learned this week and how God has worked in your heart and share with others about the relationship you have with God. Take time to thank God that He made the way for us to have a relationship with Him!

Remember It:

Memorize Romans 10:9.

> *because, if you confess with your mouth that Jesus is Lord and believe in your heart that God raised him from the dead, you will be saved.*

Romans 10:9 ESV

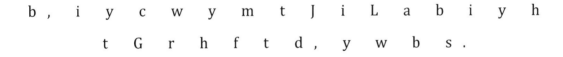

b, i y c w y m t J i L a b i y h

t G r h f t d, y w b s .

_____ _____ : _____

The "Romans Road"

Romans 3:23

" For all have sinned and fall short of the glory of God."

Romans 3:10

" As it is written: 'There is no one righteous, not even one;'"

Romans 6:23 (NLT)

" For the wages of sin is death, but the free gift of God is eternal life in Christ Jesus our Lord."

Romans 5:8

" But God demonstrates his own love for us in this: While we were still sinners, Christ died for us."

Romans 10:9-10

" If you declare with your mouth, " Jesus is Lord," and believe in your heart that God raised him from the dead, you will be saved. For it is with your heart that you believe and are justified, and it is with your mouth that you profess your faith and are saved."

Romans 10:13

" For, 'Everyone who calls on the name of the Lord will be saved.'"

Romans 5:1 (NLT)

" Therefore, since we have been made right in God's sight by faith, we have peace with God because of what Jesus Christ our Lord has done for us."

Romans 8:1-2

" Therefore, there is now no condemnation for those who are in Christ Jesus, because through Christ Jesus the law of the Spirit who gives life has set you free from the law of sin and death."

Romans 8:38-39 (NLT)

" And I am convinced that nothing can ever separate us from God's love. Neither death nor life, neither angels nor demons, neither our fears for today nor our worries about tomorrow--not even the powers of hell can separate us from God's love. No power in the sky above or in the earth below--indeed, nothing in all creation will ever be able to separate us from the love of God that is revealed in Christ Jesus our Lord."

Optional Activities

Day 1:

- Make palm leaf crosses, using palm fronds.

- Using green construction paper, trace your child's hand. Cut out and glue to a large craft stick. Use these "palm leaves" as you re-enact the triumphal entry, calling on Jesus, "Hosanna! Save us, Jesus!"

Day 2:

Make a visual reminder of how we can honor God when we go to church:

- Using craft sticks and glue, make a mini model of the church.

    o Glue four craft sticks together, forming a square.

    o Glue two additional craft sticks in the shape of a triangle, forming a roof to the church.

    o Form a cross at the peak of your triangle (roof) using two more craft sticks.

- Brainstorm 6 ways we can honor God in our behavior when we go to church.

    o On the crossbeam of the cross, write, "I honor God at church when I"

    o Write those 6 ideas on the sides of the church (square) and the roof (triangle).

- Hang this on the refrigerator or keep in your car to review each Sunday before going to church. Remember, though, it's not just about our outer actions, but the attitude of our hearts!

Day 3:

- Print, cut out, and color the templates of a trunk, tree top, and fruit included at the end of this book.

- Paste strips of blue and green construction paper against a piece of black construction paper (see image below), and paste your tree and fruit onto the scene.

- Using a crayon, draw roots from the tree deep into the soil (black construction paper). Along each root, write an idea for how we abide in Christ (reading our Bibles, memorizing Scripture, prayer, etc.)

- Write a fruit of the Spirit (Gal. 5:22) on each piece of fruit to show that it is only when we abide in Christ that this sweet fruit will grow!

Day 4:

Create a Reminder {Option 1}:

- Using the template at the end of this book, cut out the inside of both perfume bottles.

- Glue scraps of tissue paper across the back of the bottle (or cover with clear contact paper and stick the pieces of tissue paper to the contact paper). Optional: we added a solid sheet of yellow tissue paper as backing behind our strips to reinforce the center.

- Line the second bottle up against the one with tissue paper and glue the two bottles together.

- Allow to dry, then cut out and hang up!

Create a Reminder {Option 2}:

- Tear strips of tissue paper and wrap the pieces around empty baby food jars or small, glass mason jars. Using a paint brush, brush Mod Podge across the top of the tissue paper. Allow the jars to dry and spray with a clear laquer.

- Use the jars all year long to collect coins to give as a tithe, to share with someone in need, or to support a missionary!

Day 5:

- Brainstorm a list of practical ways your family can serve others. Write each idea on a separate jumbo craft stick.

- Cut, color and decorate the patterns of feet at the end of this book and glue one to each craft stick.

- Put the collection of craft sticks in a small pail, cup, or box. Choose one each day or once a week and do it!

Day 6:

- Make a lamb to remind kids that Jesus is our Passover Lamb.

- Cover a paper plate with a generous amount of liquid glue.

- Start in the center and completely cover the plate with cotton balls.

- Using black construction paper, cut a head and an ear. Glue the ear and a google eye to the head and glue the head on the back of the plate.
- Cut out two legs and glue these to the plate as well.

Day 7:

Easter Story Cookies (to be made before bedtime on the eve of Resurrection Sunday)

- Ingredients
    - 1 c. whole pecans
    - 1 tsp. vinegar
    - 3 egg whites
    - pinch of salt
    - 1 c. sugar
- Supplies
    - Ziploc bag
    - Wooden Spoon
    - Wax paper
    - Cookie Sheet
    - Tape
    - Bible
- Directions
    - Preheat oven to 300°F.
    - Put pecans in Ziploc baggy and let the children beat them with a wooden spoon, breaking the pecans into small pieces.

Explain that after Jesus was arrested, the Roman soldiers beat Him. **Read** John 19:1-3.

    - Pour 1 tsp. vinegar in mixing bowl.

Let each child smell the vinegar. Explain that when Jesus was on the cross, He was thirsty and was given vinegar to drink. **Read** John 19:28-30.

o   Add egg whites to vinegar.

Eggs represent life. Explain that Jesus gave His life to give us life. **Read** John 10:10-11.

o   Sprinkle a pinch of salt into child's hand. Let her taste it and brush the rest into the bowl.

Explain that the salt represents the salty tears shed by Jesus' followers and the bitterness of our own sin. **Read** Luke 23:27.

If you tasted the ingredients now, you'd find that they don't taste good at all!

o   Add 1 c. sugar.

Explain that the sweetest part of the story is that Jesus died because He loves us. He wants us to know and belong to Him. **Read** Psalm 34:8 and John 3:16.

o   Beat with a mixer on high speed for 12 to 15 minutes until stiff peaks are formed.

Explain that the color white represents purity. When Jesus cleanses us of our sins, we become pure in God's eyes. **Read** Isaiah1:18 and John 3:1-3.

o   Fold in broken nuts. Drop by teaspoons onto a wax paper covered cookie sheet.

Explain that each mound represents the rocky tomb where Jesus' body was laid. **Read** Matthew 27:57-60.

o   Put the cookie sheet in the oven. Close the door and turn the oven OFF.

o   Give each child a piece of tape and seal the oven door.

Explain that Jesus' tomb was sealed. **Read** Matthew 27:65-66.

o   GO TO BED!

Explain that they may feel sad to leave the cookies in the oven overnight. Jesus' followers were in despair when the tomb was sealed. **Read** John 16:20 & 22.

On Easter morning, open the oven and give everyone a cookie. Notice the cracked surface and take a bite. The cookies are hollow!

On the first Easter, Jesus' followers were amazed to find the tomb open and empty. **Read** Matthew 28:1-9.

HE HAS RISEN!

Day 8:

- Using large craft paper or construction paper, create a "He is Risen" banner. Considering drawing or including a reminder from each day this week to help retell the story of the last week of Jesus' life. Hang this banner in a prominent place in your home.

Add in your Own Activities!

_____

_____

_____

_____

_____

_____

_____

_____

_____

Supply List

Day 1:

Put it into Action:

- coats
- costumes {optional}

Optional Extra Activities:

- green construction paper
- large craft sticks
- glue
- crayons
- scissors

Day 2:

Put it into Action:

- Bibles, journal, small lamp, music, and anything else you'd like to use to create a cozy worship corner in your home

Extra Activities:

- large craft sticks
- glue
- paint, crayons, or markers

Day 3:

Put it into Action:

- large bowl
- tall drinking glass or mason jar
- small drinking glasses (1/child)
- food coloring

Create a Reminder:

- tree templates
- blue, green, black construction paper
- glue
- crayons
- scissors

Day 4:

Put it into Action:

- No supplies needed

Create a Reminder:

- perfume bottle template {option 1}
- tissue paper {option 1}
- scissors {option 1}
- glue {option 1}
- clear contact paper {optional} {option 1}
- empty baby food jars or clear mason jars {option 2}
- tissue paper {option 2}
- Mod Podge {option 2}
- Acrylic Coating Spray {option 2}

Day 5:

Put it into Action:

- Basin or bowl filled with warm soapy water
- washcloth, towel, lotion

Create a Reminder:

- large craft sticks
- feet template
- crayons
- scissors
- glue
- permanent marker

Day 6:

Put it into Action:

- wood scraps {option 1}
- paper scraps {option 1}
- pins or nails {option 1}
- rocks from outside or river rocks, like these {option 2}
- permanent marker {option 2}
- piece of red cloth {option 2}
- basket {option 2}

Create a Reminder:

- paper plate
- glue
- cotton balls
- black construction paper
- googly eye
- scissors

Day 7:

Put it into Action:

- toilet paper {option 1}
- dirty window or dirty mirror {option 2}
- glass cleaner and a rag {option 2}

Create a Reminder:

- 1 cup whole pecans
- vinegar
- 3 egg whites
- salt
- 1 cup sugar
- ziploc bag
- wooden spoon
- wax paper
- cookie sheet
- tape

Day 8:

Put it into Action:

- candy-filled Easter eggs and one empty egg {option 1}
- baked Easter story cookies from yesterday {option 2}

Create a Reminder:

- construction paper
- markers, crayons, glitter, stickers, miscellaneous craft supplies
- permanent marker

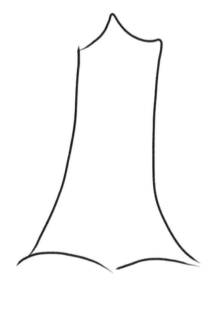

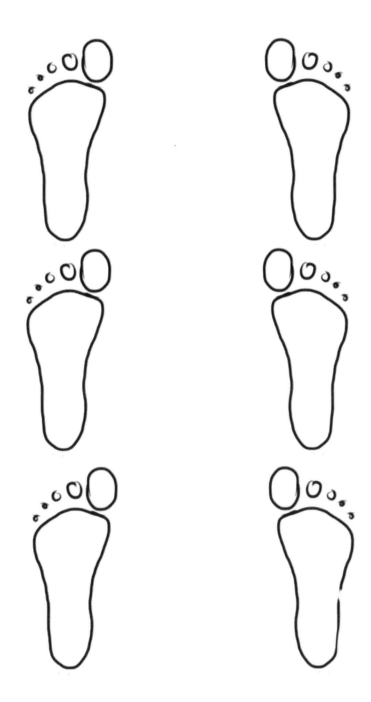

Dear Friend,

What an honor to join you here on these pages as you sought the Lord this year! I pray that this devotional helped move your hearts closer to Jesus. What a mighty God we serve!

I would love to read your feedback - would you consider sending me your story? How did this devotional impact you and your family? E-mail me at erika@faithfulmoms.org to let me know.

Please also let me know any suggestions you might have to help improve this resource!

If you're looking for other resources to help you and your family grow in faith + faithfulness, please connect with us at the links below. What an honor it is to grow together with you!

- **Blog:** https://FaithfulMoms.org
- **Instagram:** http://instagram.com/FaithfulMoms
- **Facebook:** https://www.facebook.com/ErikaSweetingDawson

Because of grace,

Erika Dawson

Erika Dawson

Printed in Great Britain
by Amazon